CHAOS
THEORY

CHAOS THEORY

TWO ESSAYS ON MARKET ANARCHY

—— by ——

ROBERT P. MURPHY

SECOND EDITION

LvMI

MISES INSTITUTE

All men with honor are kings. But not all kings have honor.
—Rob Roy (Liam Neeson)

Ludwig von Mises Institute
518 West Magnolia Avenue
Auburn, Alabama 36832
www.mises.org

Large Print Edition published 2012 by Skyler J. Collins.
Visit: www.skylerjcollins.com.

Cover image by StockFreeImages.com.

ISBN-13: 978-1479258376
ISBN-10: 1479258377

Contents

Preface to the Second Edition

Back in late 2001, I wrote a series of articles on private law for the website anti-state.com, which featured articles and a chat forum catering to anarcho-capitalists. I then wrote an essay on private defense—meaning how a free market would handle the problem of foreign military invasion—which I submitted to Jeremy Sapienza, the editor of the website, for inclusion in his printed magazine. Jeremy wrote back that the essay was too important for a magazine with limited circulation, and urged me to turn it into a book. Thus *Chaos Theory* was born. (The title was Jeremy's idea also.)

Being an unpublished author and driven by completely unrealistic assumptions of the demand for an underground pamphlet on market anarchy, I naturally elected to self-publish the first edition of *Chaos Theory*, through RJ Communications in New York City. I was going to grad school at NYU at the time, so it was easy for me to visit their offices and see that they actually existed before sending them a check.

I combined the private law articles into a single essay mirroring the structure of the private defense piece, and I arranged for Robert Vroman—another anarcho-capitalist in his 20s—to do the terrific artwork. The physical book was available by May, 2002. I can't remember the exact number of copies I had printed up—I believe it was 1,500—but I can state with certainty that I didn't think it would take almost eight years to sell them all!

Even though the country was not swept with a libertarian Great Awakening as I had hoped, it's still encouraging that we are now in a position to issue a second edition of the book. Although my own views have matured since its original publication, I still think the essays are a good introduction to someone who wonders, "How the heck could the free market provide police and defense services?!"

I consciously tried to keep the arguments in the book very practical, so that they would appeal to the widest range of readers. Most of the other introductions to anarcho-capitalism first argue for a particular value system, based on Objectivism, utilitarianism, or natural rights. Although a deep thinker needs to explore the philosophical under-pinnings of his judgments, I thought these higher questions were actually irrelevant to the main issues in *Chaos Theory*.

When it comes down to it, I think just about everybody agrees it would be nice if we could live in a society without the systematic theft of taxation or large standing armies. The problem is not one of principle so much as one of pragmatism: Most people believe (incorrectly) that the government simply *must* provide law and defense services, lest civilization itself collapse.

Rereading the essays now, the only serious shortcoming I see (given the constraints I faced) is that I jumped into the details of the operation of a market-based system of private law, without realizing exactly what it was that private judges really do. Whether or not people have signed contracts beforehand or even met each other, disputes will arise and individuals who have a reputation for honesty, fairness, and wisdom serve an important function in adjudicating or refereeing these disputes.

Stripped to its essentials, a system of private law means that people who can't come to an agreement on their own will literally seek *the opinion* of a third party. Of course, in a modern Western economy, truly private legal systems would lead to specialized training and contractual codifications of the judge's role in render-ing opinions on the cases brought before him or her. Yet the essence of the judge would remain the same as in a more primitive setting:

The judge's job would be to opine on what "the law" had to say about a particular dispute, whether the law was understood as tribal customs passed down over the generations, or instead as a web of voluntary contracts and profitable practices as they spontaneously evolved in a modern capitalist society.

One final point I want to clarify is that I am not here taking a position on the proper scope for *a priori* constructions of legal theory, versus a more open-ended "the right law is whatever the market says it is" approach of some other thinkers in this area. I am sketching the market forces that operate one step above this level of analysis. For an analogy, an economist can discuss the market for geometry textbooks without explicitly taking a stand on whether Euclid's proofs are "really" universally valid or if they instead are popular only because they are useful for building bridges and other engineering tasks. In the same way, as an economist I can explain the advantages of a private, competitive legal system versus a coercive government system, without delving into the difficult question of what the ideal legal code would look like—or if such a thing even exists. These are important issues, to be sure, but I think they are tangential to the case for private law.

With these clarifications in mind, I hope the reader will enjoy the following essays. In my experience, once we simply imagine the possibility of a society without the State, the case for anarcho-capitalism or "market anarchy" seems obvious.

Robert P. Murphy
December 2009

Illustration: Robert Vroman

Private Law[1]

W ithout question, the legal system is the one facet of society that supposedly requires State provision. Even such champions of laissez-faire as Milton Friedman and Ludwig von Mises believed a government must exist to protect private property and define the "rules of the game."

However, their arguments focused on the necessity of law itself. They simply assumed that the market is incapable of defining and protecting property rights. They were wrong.

In this essay, I argue that the elimination of the State will *not* lead to lawless chaos. Voluntary institutions will emerge to effectively and peacefully[2] resolve the disputes arising in everyday life. Not only will market law be more *efficient*, it will also be more *equitable*, than the government alternative.

Just as right-wing hawks embrace the Orwellian notion that War is Peace, left-wing egalitarians believe that Slavery is Freedom.[3] The hawks wage endless war to end war, while the social democrats engage in massive theft—or "taxation" as they call it—to eliminate crime.

---

[1] This essay is based on three articles originally featured on anti-state.com.

[2] More accurately, disputes will be handled *relatively* peacefully; force may occasionally be required. Although market anarchism is thus not pacifism, we note that true pacifism—the refusal to engage in violence—implies anarchism, since all State action is based on (the threat of) violence.

[3] In the original, "FREEDOM IS SLAVERY." George Orwell, *1984* (New York: Signet Classics, 1984), p. 7.

It is high time to abandon such monstrous paradoxes. It took no king to produce language, money, or science, and it takes no government to produce a just legal system.

I. CONTRACT

First, we must abandon the idea of a mythical "law of the land." There doesn't need to be a single set of laws binding everyone. In any event, such a system never existed. The laws in each of the fifty states are different, and the difference in legal systems between countries is even more pronounced. Yet we go about our daily lives, and even visit and do business with foreign nations, without too much trouble.

All actions in a purely free society[4] would be subject to *contract*. For example, it is currently a crime to steal, because the legislature says so. A prospective employer knows that if I steal from his firm, he can notify the government and it will punish me.

But in a stateless society there wouldn't be a legislated body of laws, nor would there be government courts or police. Nonetheless, employers would still like some protection from theft by their employees. So before hiring an applicant, the employer would make him sign a document[5] that had clauses to the effect of, "I promise not to steal from the Acme Firm. If I get caught stealing, *as established by Arbitration Agency X*, then I agree to pay whatever restitution that Agency X deems appropriate."

---

[4] A *free* society is one in which property rights are (generally) respected. The existence of a State—an institution that uses force to place itself *above* property rights—thus precludes *freedom* as we shall use the term.

[5] I hasten to note that the system of market law that I describe is not entirely congruent with the vision of some other anarcho-capitalist writers. They believe the "just" system of property rights is deducible axiomatically, and that objectively valid law will be discovered and enforced by private firms. For an excellent introduction, see Linda and Morris Tannehill, *The Market for Liberty* (New York: Laissez-Faire Books, 1984); and Murray N. Rothbard, *For a New Liberty* (New York: Collier, 1978).

We immediately see two things in this contract. First, it is completely voluntary; any "laws" binding the employee have been acknowledged by him, beforehand. Second, the existence of Arbitration Agency X ensures fairness and objectivity in any disputes.

To see this, suppose that it didn't. Suppose that a big firm bribed the arbitrators at Agency X, so that lazy workers (who were going to be fired anyway) were (falsely) charged by the employers with embezzlement, while Agency X always ruled "guilty." With this scheme, the big firm could bilk thousands of dollars from its bad employees before terminating them. And since the hapless employees had agreed beforehand to abide by the arbitration outcome, they could do nothing about it.[6]

But upon consideration, it's easy to see that such behavior would be foolish. Just because an arbitration agency ruled a certain way, wouldn't make everyone *agree* with it, just as people complain about outrageous court rulings by *government* judges. The press would pick up on the unfair rulings, and people would lose faith in the objectivity of Agency X's decisions. Potential employees would think twice before working for the big firm, as long as it required (in its work contracts) that people submitted to the suspect Agency X.

Other firms would patronize different, more reputable arbitration agencies, and workers would flock to them. Soon enough, the corrupt big firm and Arbitration Agency X would suffer huge financial penalties for their behavior.

Under market anarchy, *all* aspects of social intercourse would be "regulated" by voluntary contracts. Specialized firms would probably provide standardized forms so that new contracts wouldn't have to be drawn up every time people did business. For example, if a customer bought something on installment, the store would probably have him sign a form that said something to the effect,

---

[6] An appeals process might be included in the arbitration procedure, but then the big firm could just bribe *those* judges, too.

"I agree to the provisions of the 2002 edition Standard Deferred Payment Procedures as published by the Ace legal firm."

Expertise

Under this system, legal experts would draft the "laws of the land," *not* corrupt and inept politicians. And these experts would be chosen in open competition with all rivals. Right now one can buy "definitive" style manuals for writing term papers, or dictionaries of the English language. The government doesn't need to establish the "experts" in these fields. It would be the same way with private legal contracts. Everybody knows the "rules" of grammar just like everyone would know what's "legal" and what isn't.

Murder

Of course, one of the most basic stipulations in any contractual relationship—whether entering a mall or living in a neighborhood co-op—would be strong prohibitions on murder. In other words *all* contracts of this type would have a clause saying, "If I am found guilty of murder I agree to pay $y million to the estate of the deceased." Naturally, no one would *sign* such a contract unless he were sure that the trial procedures used to determine his guilt or innocence had a strong presumption of innocence; nobody would want to be found guilty of a murder he didn't commit. But on the other hand, the procedures would have to be designed so that there were still a good chance that *guilty* people would actually be convicted, since people don't want to shop in malls where murder goes unpunished.

And, because *all* contracts of this sort (except possibly in very eccentric areas frequented by people who liked to live dangerously) would contain such clauses, one could say that "murder is illegal" in the whole anarchist society, even though the evidentiary rules and penalties might differ from area to area. But this is no different from our *current* system,[7] and no one doubts that "murder is illegal" in the current United States.

Profitability the Standard

The beauty of this system is that the competing desires of everyone are taken into account. The market solves this problem everyday, in reference to other goods and services. For example, it would be very convenient for customers if a deli were open twenty-four hours a day. But on the other hand, such long shifts would be very tedious for its *workers*. So the market system of profit and loss determines the "correct" hours of operation.

In the same way, we saw above how evidentiary rules would be determined under a system of private law. Because people would be submitting themselves contractually to the rulings of a certain arbitration agency, the agency would need a reputation for objectivity and fairness to defendants. But on the other hand, the owners of stores, firms, rental cars, etc. would want some means of restitution in the event of theft, and so the arbitration agencies couldn't be *too* lenient. As with the hours of a store's operation, so too would the legal procedures be decided by the profit and loss test. Maybe there would be juries, maybe there wouldn't. We can't predict this beforehand, just as we can't say *a priori* how many tricycles "should" be made this year; we let the market take care of it, automatically.

II. INSURANCE

The contractual system described above seems to work well, except for one nagging problem: How can people afford to *pay* these outrageous fines? Granted, someone might sign a piece of paper, pledging restitution to his employer if he is caught stealing.

---

[7] For example, only some states have the death penalty.

But suppose he steals anyway, and is found guilty by the arbitration agency, but has no money. Then what?

Well, how does our present system of auto damages work? Right now, if I sideswipe someone, I must pay a stiff penalty. Or rather, my *insurance company* does.

It would be the same way with *all* torts and crimes under the system I've described. An insurance company would act as a guarantor (or co-signer) of a client's contracts with various firms. Just as a bank uses experts to take depositors' money and efficiently allocate it to borrowers, so too would the experts at the insurance company determine the risk of a certain client (i.e., the likelihood he or she would violate contracts by stealing or killing) and charge an appropriate premium. Thus, other firms wouldn't have to keep tabs on all of their customers and employees; the firms' only responsibility would be to make sure everyone they dealt with carried a policy with a reputable insurance agency.

Under this system, the victims of a crime are always paid, immediately. (Contrast this to the government system, where victims usually get nothing except the satisfaction of seeing the criminal placed behind bars.) There would also be incentives for people to behave responsibly. Just as reckless drivers pay higher premiums for car insurance, so too would repeat offenders be charged higher premiums for their contract insurance.

And why would the person with criminal proclivities *care* about his insurance company? Well, if he stopped paying his premiums, his coverage would be dropped. With no one to underwrite his contractual obligations, such a person would make a very poor customer or employee. People wouldn't hire him or trust him to browse through a china shop, since there would be no "legal" recourse if he did anything "criminal." In order to get by in society, it would be extremely useful to keep one's insurance coverage by always paying the premiums. And *that* means it would be in one's great interest to refrain from criminal activity, since that would be the way to keep premiums down.

Admittedly, such arguments seem fanciful. But they are no more farfetched than the modern credit card system. People have huge lines of credit advanced to them, sometimes only by filling out a form, and it is extremely easy to engage in credit card fraud. A prodigal may run up a huge bill and simply refuse to pay it, yet in most cases nothing physical will happen to him. But most people *don't* behave in such an irresponsible manner, because they don't want to ruin their credit history. If they do, they know they'll forever more be cut off from this wonderful tool of the capitalist society.

III. PRISON

We have now established that a system of voluntary, contractual law can be imagined theoretically, and would even work in a society populated with self-interested but ultimately rational people.

But what about the really tough cases? What about the incorrigible bank robber, or the crazed ax murderer? Surely there will always be deviant, antisocial individuals who, through malice or ignorance, ignore the incentives and commit crimes. How would a system of market anarchy deal with such people?

First, keep in mind that wherever someone is standing in a purely libertarian[8] society, he would be on somebody's property. This is the way in which force could be brought to bear on criminals without violating their natural rights.

For example, the contract[9] of a movie theater would have a clause to the effect, "If I am judged guilty of a crime by a reputable arbi-

---

[8] In this context, *libertarian* implies a respect for "natural" rights. The libertarian's ultimate credo is the non-aggression axiom, namely that it is illegitimate to initiate force. Although market anarchy (as I will describe it) does not rest upon libertarianism, I will argue that it is (largely) consistent with this philosophy. Divergences between the two are, I believe, points of weakness in the libertarian position.

[9] Even if it weren't literally signed every visit, the agreement would be understood implicitly.

tration agency [perhaps listed in an Appendix], I release the theater owner from any liability should armed men come to remove me from his property."

So we see that it is not a contradiction to use force to capture fugitives in a completely voluntary society. All such uses would have been authorized by the recipients themselves beforehand.[10]

But where would these ne'er-do-wells be taken, once they were brought into "custody"? Specialized firms would develop, offering high security analogs to the current jailhouse. However, the "jails" in market anarchy would compete with each other to *attract criminals*.

Consider: No insurance company would vouch for a serial killer if he applied for a job at the local library, but they *would* deal with him if he agreed to live in a secure building under close scrutiny. The insurance company would make sure that the "jail" that held him was well-run. After all, if the person escaped and killed again, the insurance company would be held liable, since it pledges to make good on any damages its clients commit.

On the other hand, there would be no undue cruelty for the prisoners in such a system. Although they would have no chance of escape (unlike government prisons), they wouldn't be beaten by sadistic guards. If they were, they'd simply switch to a different jail, just as travelers can switch hotels if they view the staff as discourteous. Again, the insurance company (which vouches for a violent person) doesn't care *which* jail its client chooses, so long as its inspectors have determined that the jail will not let its client escape into the general population.

---

[10] Of course, if someone tried to simply barge onto another's property, without agreeing to any contractual obligations, then the owner would be perfectly justified in using force to repel him. Although this default may seem unilateral, it would at least be codified and publicized. Later sections will deal with the problem of initially drawing up property boundaries.

IV. DOUBTS

Although superficially coherent and workable, the proposed system of market law will certainly engender skepticism. In the interest of brevity, I will deal with some common (and valid) concerns.[11]

"What about someone who has no insurance?"

If an individual didn't carry insurance, other people would have no guaranteed recourse should the individual damage or steal their property. Such an individual would therefore be viewed with suspicion, and people would be reluctant to deal with him except for single transactions involving small sums. He would probably be unable to get a full-time job, a bank loan, or a credit card. Many residential and commercial areas would probably require that all visitors carried valid policies before allowing them to even enter.[12]

So we see that those without insurance would have their options, including their freedom of movement, greatly restricted. At the same time, the premiums for basic contract insurance, at least for people without a criminal history, would be quite low.[13] So there

---

[11] Many of these points were inspired by fruitful discussion with Matt Lasley, David Pinholster, Chris Redwood, Stephen Carville, Stephan Kinsella, and Dan Mahoney. However, the objections do not necessarily reflect the views of these thinkers.

[12] Such a statement brings to mind the horrors of identification papers and checkpoints. However, State abuses should not discredit the valid concerns of property owners. As argued most notably by Hans Hermann Hoppe, individuals do not possess an inherent "freedom of movement." If owners wish to restrict the people who travel on their roads, that is entirely their prerogative. On the other hand, in an established anarchist society, customers wouldn't show ID every time they entered most stores, just as in our present society people don't draw up labor contracts every time they hire the neighbor's kid to mow the lawn.

[13] To repeat: under this system everybody would buy homicide insurance, just as right now surgeons buy medical malpractice insurance; the insurance company is pledging to compensate the estate of anyone killed by its

wouldn't be very many people walking around without this type of insurance. It's true, some people would still commit crimes and would have no insurance company to pay damages, but such cases are going to occur under *any* legal system.

Furthermore, once someone (without insurance) *had* committed a serious crime, he would still be chased by detectives, just as he would be under the government system. And if these (far more efficient) private detectives found him at any time on a normal piece of property, they would have the full right to arrest him.[14]

Warring Agencies

Critics often dismiss private law by alleging that disputes between enforcement agencies would lead to combat—even though this happens between governments all the time! In truth, the incentives for peaceful resolution of disputes would be far greater in market anarchy than the present system. Combat is very *expensive*, and private companies take much better care of their assets than government officials take care of their subjects' lives and property.

In any event, those engaging in "warfare" in a free society would be treated as any other murderers. Unlike government soldiers, private mercenaries would receive no special privileges to engage in condoned violence. Those agencies *interpreting* the law would not be the same as the firms *enforcing* it. There is no intrinsic reason

---

clients. Because the probability of an individual (with no prior record) being convicted of murder in the next year is very small, his premium would also be small. If the company's actuaries estimate that a potential client has, say, only a one in a million chance of killing in the next year, and the standard damages for murder are, say, $10 million, then the company would only need to charge roughly $10 per year to break even.

[14] As explained in section III, most property would have a clause in which all guests *agreed* to submit to arrest if the guests were "wanted" by a reputable arbitration agency.

to worry about battles between private enforcement agencies,[15] any more than battles between the government army and navy.

"Won't the Mafia take over?"

It is paradoxical that the fear of rule by organized crime families causes people to support the State, which is the most "organized" and criminal association in human history. Even if it were true that under market anarchy, people had to pay protection money and occasionally get whacked, this would be a drop in the bucket compared to the taxation and wartime deaths caused by governments.

But even this concedes too much. For the mob derives its strength from *government*, not the free market. All of the businesses traditionally associated with organized crime—gambling, prostitution, loan sharking, drug dealing—are prohibited or heavily regulated by the State.[16] In market anarchy, true professionals would drive out such unscrupulous competitors.

"Your insurance companies would become the State!"

On the contrary, the private companies providing legal services would have far less power under market anarchy than the government currently possesses. Most obvious, there would be no power to tax or to monopolize "service." If a particular insurance company were reluctant to pay legitimate claims, this would become quickly

---

[15] This statement does not hold for the systems of private law (elaborated by other anarcho-capitalists) in which agencies unilaterally punish anyone harming their clients. In such a system, the lack of a monopolist *would* create an additional theoretical problem for the advocate of private defense agencies. However, even here the incentives for a peaceful resolution of legitimate disputes are tremendous.

[16] The mob is also strengthened by unions, which (in their modern form) are anything but voluntary organizations.

known, and people would take this into account when dealing with clients of this disreputable firm.[17]

The fear that (under market anarchy) private individuals would replace politicians, overlooks the true causes of State mischief. Unlike feudal monarchs, democratic rulers don't actually *own* the resources (including human) that they control. Furthermore, the duration of their rule (and hence control of these resources) is very uncertain. For these reasons, politicians and other government employees do not exercise much care in maintaining the (market) value of the property in their jurisdiction. Shareholders of a private company, however, have every interest in choosing personnel and policies to maximize the profitability of the firm.

All the horrors of the State—onerous taxation, police brutality, total war—are not only monstrous, but they're also grossly *inefficient*. It would never be profitable for anarchist insurance and legal firms to mimic the policies set by governments.[18]

Children

The question of children is one of the most difficult. As a first pass, let us note that, obviously, concerned parents would only

---

[17] It may be true that currently, insurance companies are bureaucratic and overbearing. But I think this has more to do with their close relationship with the *government* legal system, rather than with their nature as such. Yes, insurance companies don't like paying damages, but people don't like going to work everyday, either. This doesn't mean the free labor market isn't a viable system; if people are lazy, they get fired. And if an insurance company doesn't pay its claims, it will eventually go out of business.

[18] For the sake of argument, let us suppose (quite implausibly) that everyone agreed to sell his or her land to a single individual, who then became landlord of the entire population, and that as part of the lease, everyone agreed to give the landlord the power to "tax" earnings. Even so, this landlord would never set the tax rate above the "Laffer point," i.e., the point that maximized revenues. Because it is influenced by non-pecuniary motives, however, the modern State doesn't respect even this sensible rule.

patronize those schools, and live in those apartments or housing complexes, where the protection of their children was of paramount importance to the staff.

Beyond this, the basic "prohibitions" on parental child abuse and neglect could be stipulated in the marriage contract. In addition to whatever romance may be entailed, a marriage is ultimately a partnership between two people, and prudent couples will officially spell out this arrangement, with all of its benefits and obligations. For example, before abandoning her career to raise a man's children, a woman may require a financial pledge in case of divorce (i.e., dissolving the partnership). In the same way, a standard clause in marriage contracts could define and specify penalties for the improper treatment of children.[19]

Another point to consider is the enhanced role of adoption in a free society. Much as it shocks modern sensibilities, there would be a fully functioning "baby market," in which parental privileges were sold to the highest bidder.[20] Although seemingly crass, such a market would surely reduce child abuse. After all, abusive or negligent parents are probably the ones most likely to offer their children for adoption, when loving couples are allowed to pay them handsomely for it.[21]

---

[19] This device only works, of course, if at least one of the partners is concerned for the welfare of future children. Yet this should be sufficient for most cases, since surely very few couples dream of becoming abusive parents.

[20] I am purposefully skirting the question of whether parents would legally "own" their children. So long as a child voluntarily remained with his parents, "living under their roof," they could of course set any rules they wished. The only problem arises when a child runs away, and does not wish to return. I personally am sympathetic to the notion that so long as a child can support him or herself, parents can't force the child to return home.

[21] These voluntary solutions would be far preferable to the government approach, in which ill-informed and often self-righteous "social workers" rip families apart and place children in the horrible foster care system.

The controversial issue of abortion, just as other conflicts in a private law system, would be handled by competing firms setting policies to best match the desires of their customers. Those people sufficiently horrified by the practice could establish a gated community in which all residents agreed to refrain from abortion, and to report anyone caught performing one.[22]

Title Registry

In market anarchy, who would define property rights? If someone hands over the money to purchase a house, what guarantees does he have?

This is a complex issue, and I won't be able to give specifics, since the actual market solution would depend on the circumstances of the case and would draw on the legal expertise (far greater than mine) of the entire community.[23] I can, however, offer some general remarks.

Whatever (if any) the abstract or metaphysical nature of property law, the purpose of public *titles* is quite utilitarian; they are necessary to allow individuals to effectively plan and coordinate their interactions with each other. Specialized firms (perhaps distinct from arbitration agencies) would keep records on the property titles, either for a specific area or group of individuals. Title registry would probably be accomplished through a complex, hierarchical web of such firms.[24]

---

[22] This would not prevent others from forming a community in which abortion were legal, of course.

[23] My stance may appear slippery, but imagine that a Cuban economist advises Castro to abolish socialism and allow a free market to develop. Must the economist predict beforehand whether and how many shopping malls will exist under his proposal?

[24] For example, one firm might issue land titles for an entire city, but actually delegate the delimitation of the respective rights of two neighbors to a *different* firm specializing in residential affairs.

The fear of rogue agencies, unilaterally declaring themselves "owner" of everything, is completely unfounded. In market anarchy, the companies publicizing property rights would not be the same as the companies *enforcing* those rights. More important, competition between firms would provide *true* "checks and balances." If one firm began flouting the community norms established and codified on the market, it would go out of business, just as surely as a manufacturer of dictionaries would go broke if its books contained improper definitions.

Infinite Regress

A sophisticated critic may charge that my proposal rests upon a circular argument: How can people use contracts to define property rights, when a system of property rights is necessary to determine which contracts are valid? After all, Smith can't sell Jones a car for a certain sum of money, unless it is established *beforehand* that Smith is the just owner of the car (and Jones the owner of the sum of money).[25]

To see the solution, we must break the problem into two parts. First, we should ask, "Could the free market provide a foundation for social interaction?" I believe the previous sections have demonstrated this. That is, I have shown above that *if we had a system of property titles recognized by competing firms*, then a contractual system governing the exchange of those titles would form a stable basis for private law.

Now, it is an entirely different question to ask, "How are these titles *initially* defined and allocated?" This is a broad topic, and will be addressed in the next section. But to deal with the issue as it relates to the alleged infinite regress, let us consider contract law.

---

[25] The knowledgeable reader may notice that this objection—and its solution—are similar to the alleged infinite regress involved in a marginal utility explanation of money demand.

Contract law is a specific branch of law, much as tort law or constitutional law. It is used, for example, to determine whether a contract between two parties is legally binding. Now surely *contract* law can't be established in an anarchist system of *contractual* law, for wouldn't this beg the question?

No. The contractual pledges made by individuals would contain provisions for all of the contingencies handled by today's contract law. For example, the insurance company backing up a customer would be promising, "We will make good on any debts that our client fails to pay, *so long as the obligations have been spelled out in a valid contract*, according to the terms described in the Standard Contract Law pamphlet published by the Ace legal firm."

This pamphlet would perhaps require signatures in black ink, notarized oversight for large sums, and that the signers to a contract were of sufficient age and sobriety, and were not under duress, when the contract was made.[26] As with all elements of private law, the precise rules governing contract interpretation would be determined by the (possibly conflicting) desires of everyone through the profit and loss test.

Finally, keep in mind that the *ultimate* judge in a given case is…the judge. No matter how voluminous the law books, or how obvious the precedents, every case will ultimately depend

---

[26] The purist might object that this remedy is insufficient. After all, I am simply assuming that people know what the *concept* of a contract is. To this charge I plead guilty. As mentioned in the Foreword, my purpose in this essay is not to "prove" the ethical superiority of market law. Despite the occasional normative statement, I am really just describing the world I envision under market anarchy. And in such a world, I do not predict that people will have trouble adopting the convention of contracts (even without a proper philosophical definition and justification), just as I don't predict they will need to be versed in economic theory before using money.

on the subjective interpretation of an arbiter or judge who must deliver the ruling.[27]

We must never forget that written statutes as such are powerless unless used by competent and equitable individuals. Only in a competitive, voluntary system is there any hope for judicial excellence.

"How do we get there?"

The route to a free society will vary according to the history of a region, and consequently no single description will do. The path taken by North Korean market anarchists will no doubt differ from the course of similarly minded individuals in the United States. In the former, violent overthrow of unjust regimes may occur, while in the latter, a gradual and orderly erosion of the State is a wonderful possibility. The one thing all such revolutions would share is a commitment by the overwhelming majority to a *total respect* of property rights.

All societies, no matter how despotic their rulers, must possess a basic degree of respect for property rights, even if such respect is given due to custom rather than intellectual appreciation. All people know that it is a crime to rape or murder;[28] even rapists and murderers know this.

Such universal, intuitive notions of justice would constitute the foundation for a system of private law. This widespread agreement would allow for more specific, contractually defined rights to evolve.[29] The process would be continuous, with one stage of

---

[27] In a private legal system, there still would be publicized laws and adherence to precedent, for this would allow greater predictability in rulings and hence appeal to customers.

[28] Of course, the major hurdle of anarchism is to convince people that murder is wrong even when duly elected "representatives" order it.

[29] To illustrate: Suppose that the distribution of this book causes every U.S. citizen to endorse market anarchism. Private firms would arise to codify the property titles that were previously regulated by government agencies. It would be "obvious" that people retained ownership of their homes (*and*

codified property titles and legal rules forming the basis for the next generation of judges and scholars to systematize and extend.

Regular people understand the waste and senselessness of conflict; they will go to great lengths and make great compromises to achieve consensus. For example, despite the lack of a formal government, newly arriving miners during the California gold rushes respected the claims of earlier settlers. To take a more modern example, even inner city toughs unthinkingly obey the "rules" in a pickup game of basketball, despite the lack of a referee.[30]

In market anarchy, free individuals, through their patronage of competing judicial and insurance firms, would foster a humane and just legal system. Those antisocial individuals who disrupted the process (by blatantly violating obvious property rights) would be dealt with in the ways described earlier.

Legal Positivism?

Some readers may wonder how I can propose a replacement for the State's "justice" system when I haven't first offered a rational theory of the source and nature of legitimate property rights.

---

mortgages), cars, etc. This basic framework of property would then allow for a voluntary, contractual solution to the more difficult problems, such as assigning titles to government housing projects (since both tenants and taxpayers might claim rightful ownership).

[30] The reader may consider this a poor example, since after all fouling is more flagrant in outdoor courts than in, say, an NBA game. But this is the point: There still is such a *thing* as a foul (and other rules) recognized by the transgressor in a pickup game; he will simply deny that he committed one. (For a different example, no player would claim that his shot should be awarded ten points.)

Now, the market solution to such ambiguity and bias, for games deemed important enough to warrant the extra cost and hassle, is to appoint official referees to apply the "law" (which they too unthinkingly respect). Notice that at no point is a violent monopoly needed to achieve this orderly outcome.

The answer is simple: I don't have such a theory. Nonetheless, I can still say that a market system of private law would work far more effectively than the State alternative, and that the standard objections to anarchy are unfounded.

There is widespread distrust of allowing the market to "determine" something as crucial as, say, prohibitions on murder. But "the market" is just shorthand for the totality of economic interactions of freely acting individuals. To allow the market to set legal rules really means that no one uses *violence* to impose his own vision on everyone else.[31]

Murder isn't wrong merely because it fails the market test; of course not. But its intrinsic immorality will find *expression* through market forces. We can all agree—contractually—to refrain from murder, and to abide by the decisions made by an arbiter should we be tried for such a crime. In this way, we know we are not violating anyone's rights.

Now, *after* we have reached such agreement and are secure in our lives, we can let the philosophers and theologians argue about *why* murder is wrong. Legal scholars offering *a priori* constructions of just law would certainly have a place in market anarchy; after all, their tracts might influence the judges' decisions. However, in this essay I focus on the market forces that will shape private law, *not* on the content of such law.[32]

---

[31] Because I am not advocating pacifism, this accusation of violence may seem hypocritical. However, the State requires the threat of violence *on admittedly innocent* people. If a person (whom everyone agrees is not a criminal) started a legal or insurance firm that infringed on the State's monopoly, it would punish him.

[32] An analogy may be useful: For a variety of reasons, I oppose public schooling and advocate its immediate abolition. I am quite confident that private schools would provide excellent education for all children, rich and poor. Now, I say this even though I cannot construct an *a priori* theory of a proper education. Nonetheless, I am confident that the market system will be *better* than the State's approach, even though I cannot list the necessary and

V. APPLICATIONS

So far I have concentrated on the crucial issues in a theoretical discussion of private law. Now I would like to illustrate the versatility of such a system in a wide variety of areas, and contrast its performance with the monopolized government alternative.

Product Safety

One of the most common charges against pure *laissez-faire* is that a completely unregulated market would leave consumers at the mercy of ruthless businessmen. We are told that without benevolent government oversight, food would be poisonous, television sets would explode, and apartment buildings would collapse.[33] It's true, such critics might concede, that in the long run, shady companies would eventually go out of business. But surely someone who sells a deadly hamburger should be immediately *punished* for this, on top of forfeiting future customers.

As with other areas of law, I believe the market would deal with these sorts of cases through contractual pledges. When a consumer bought something, part of the package would be a guarantee such as, "If this product causes injury, as determined by a reputable arbitration agency, the customer is entitled to the standard damages." And, just as individuals would likely need to be backed by a large insurance company before anyone would do business with

---

sufficient conditions of goodness (in this context). And of course, nothing *guarantees* that the market solution will be optimal; after all, if the parents in a certain town were evil or stupid, then market incentives would lead to (what we would consider) horrible curricula.

[33] I point out in passing that television sets *did* explode in the Soviet Union, and many apartment buildings *did* collapse in statist Turkey after a mild earthquake.

them, so too would businesses need to be insured against possible customer lawsuits, if they wanted to attract customers.[34]

We immediately see that this system avoids the nightmare scenarios cooked up by proponents of government regulation. Let's take the case of air travel. The Federal Aviation Administration "guarantees" that airplanes have had proper maintenance, pilots are rested, etc. So customers don't need to worry about their planes crashing. In contrast, many people allege, under a free market customers would have to keep statistics on how many crashes each airline had, and they'd have to be experts in airplane maintenance to see which companies were best.

But this is nonsense. All a flier needs to do is make sure that when he buys a plane ticket, part of what he buys is a pledge (backed by an insurance company) saying, "If you are killed in a plane crash, our airline will pay your estate $y million." Now, since the insurance companies stand to lose millions if the planes of this airline crash, it is *they* who will hire trained inspectors, keep meticulous maintenance logs, etc. They would say to the airlines: "Yes, we will underwrite your contractual pledges to customers, but *only if* you follow our safety procedures, allow our inspectors to look at your planes, work out an adequate pilot screening process, etc., and if we catch you violating your agreement, we will fine you accordingly." Since they are out to maximize profits, the insurance company will gladly pay for preventive efforts if this will lead to a greater savings in expected payments of claims to those killed in a crash.

This stands in sharp contrast to the present system. The FAA too sets up guidelines, but what are its incentives? If there is a plane crash, the FAA itself will get *more* funding, since everyone will say

---

[34] If an individual liked to live dangerously, he'd be perfectly free to buy a computer from a firm that did *not* carry insurance. But if something went wrong, it would be much more difficult for him to get his money back. It would thus be in the great interest of most people to only do business with companies that had their contracts backed by large, reputable insurance companies.

the crash shows how awful the "free market" in airplanes is. Bloated government agencies always mismanage their resources, so that there will be too many mid-level managers and not enough inspectors. Most important, since there is no *competition*, there is no benchmark against which to compare the FAA's oversight. Some lowly mechanic might have a great idea to improve airline safety, but the bureaucratic FAA would take years to implement it.

Professional Licensing

Closely related to the area of product safety is professional licensing. Let's use the example of medicine. Without government regulation, many believe, patients would be at the mercy of quacks. Ignorant consumers would go to whatever brain surgeon charged the lowest price, and would be butchered on the operating table. To prevent this, the benevolent government must establish guidelines—backed up by guns—to limit those who enter the medical profession.

This of course is nonsense. Voluntary organizations would probably arise, allowing only qualified doctors into their ranks. Concerned consumers would then patronize only those doctors endorsed by reputable associations. Before undergoing risky procedures or ingesting prescribed drugs, patients would require contractual pledges for restitution in the event of injury. In this case, it is again the insurance companies who would make sure the doctors they were underwriting were in fact qualified. Since they'd stand to lose millions in malpractice suits, the insurance companies would be very careful when setting their standards.

Such a system would be far preferable to the present one. As it is, the American Medical Association is little more than a glorified union, which requires immense schooling and training to artificially restrict the number of doctors in order to drive up their salaries (and health care costs in general). Without its monopoly, the AMA would be unable to check the growth in "alternative" therapies, such as herbal, that sidestep the current cozy alliance of big pharmaceutical companies, hospitals, and the government.

One must also realize that the incentives of the Food and Drug Administration render it far too conservative: If people die because of a new drug that the FDA has approved, the FDA will be blamed. But if people die because the FDA has *not* approved a new drug, it won't be held accountable; the sickness itself will be blamed. Consequently, many potentially life-saving drugs are currently being withheld from dying patients. In a purely free market, patients would be allowed to take whatever drugs they wanted.

Gun Control

I realize that many libertarians find certain aspects of my system a bit unnerving. Without unconditional guarantees of abstract rights, it seems there would always be a danger of smuggling the State in through the back door.

Rather than dance around such issues, I'll give the best example I can think of to demonstrate the difference between the conventional libertarian approach and my own: gun control. As we'll see, I don't think my approach is *inconsistent* with the libertarian creed, but I do think it will (at least initially) make many libertarians uncomfortable.

The standard arguments over gun control go like this: Opponents say gun control will render people defenseless against criminals and leave citizens at the mercy of their government rulers; only when someone has actually *used* his gun against innocents can the law rightfully step in. Proponents of gun control, however, argue that this position is too dogmatic; surely some preventive measures are justified in the public interest.

As with most debates held within the context of a government legal system, I think both sides have legitimate points. Certainly we cannot trust the government to protect us once it has disarmed us. But on the other hand, I feel a bit silly arguing that people should be able to stockpile atomic weapons in their basement. (A strict interpretation of many libertarian arguments would mean just that.) Fortunately, the system of private law that I've described allows us to sidestep this apparent "tradeoff."

Recall that the penalties for injury and murder would be established by contractual pledges, underwritten by insurance companies. People allow Joe Smith onto their property because they know if he hurts someone, either he will directly pay the damages or his insurance company will. The insurance company makes its money by charging appropriate premiums, tailored to the individual client. If Joe Smith has been deemed guilty in the past of violent behavior, his insurance premiums will be accordingly higher.

But there are *other* factors that an insurance company would take into account when setting premiums, besides past behavior. And one of these factors would undoubtedly be: What sort of weapons does this client keep around the house? After all, if the insurance company is going to agree to pay, say, $10 million to the estate of anyone Joe Smith kills, the company will be very interested to know whether Smith keeps sawed off shotguns—let alone atomic weapons—in his basement. Someone who keeps such weapons is much more likely to harm others, as far as the insurance company is concerned, and so his premiums will be that much higher. In fact, the risk of a client who kept nuclear (or chemical, biological, etc.) weapons would be so great that probably no policy would be offered.

This approach is superior to the governmental one. Truly dangerous weapons would be restricted to individuals willing to pay the high premiums associated with their ownership; kids couldn't buy bazookas at the local K-Mart. On the other hand, there wouldn't be the slippery slope that there is now with all *government* gun control. We would never fear that all handguns would be banned, since the insurance companies would be out strictly to make profit, and it would be far more profitable to allow people to keep handguns and pay slightly higher premiums.[35]

As with all contracts under my system, those "regulating" guns would be completely voluntary, involving no violation of libertarian rights. The insurance company is not *forcing* people to give up their bazookas. All it is saying is this: If you want us to guarantee your contracts with others, you can't own a bazooka. The insurance companies are the just owners of their money, and it is thus perfectly within their rights to make such a request.[36]

This is far preferable to the government system, which has no accountability. If politicians ban guns and cause thousands of people to be victimized by crime, nothing happens to them. But if an insurance company makes unreasonable demands of its clients, they will switch to a different company and it will quickly go out of business.

Dangerous Criminals

The supposed tradeoff between individual liberty and public safety is also exemplified in the debates over legal "technicalities." Conservatives like to complain about cases where a known murderer is set free by a bleeding heart judge, simply because the police coerced a confession or forgot to read the suspect his rights. Liberals (such as Alan Dershowitz) respond that although such cases are unfortunate, they are necessary to keep the police in line.

---

[35] In fact, households with conventional firearms might enjoy *lower* premiums, if the insurance company thinks this will reduce the incidence of crime in the area enough to justify the incentive.

[36] To charge higher premiums to those who wish to own multiple weapons is no more unjust than the present practice of offering discounts to drivers for taking a driving safety class, or to homeowners for installing an alarm system. If a particular insurance company is staffed by people who fear guns, then gun owners will shop around for a different insurance company.

As with gun control, I am sympathetic to both sides in this debate, and again I think my system can avoid both sorts of absurdities. To see this, let's suppose that through some quirk, a clearly "guilty" murderer has technically not violated any contractual provisions. Or, suppose an arbiter—who would only be *hearing* murder cases because of past excellence in his rulings—for some reason makes an outrageous ruling, and finds someone innocent of murder despite overwhelming evidence to the contrary.[37]

Because he was technically acquitted, the murderer would not have to pay damages to the estate of his victim. However, the rules governing this episode would be quickly revised to prevent its recurrence; private companies would be under much greater pressure than monopoly governments in the face of such bad publicity.

There is another difference. Under a government system, someone acquitted on a technicality gets off scot-free. But under the private law system I've described, the killer's insurance company could still increase the premiums they charged. It wouldn't matter whether their client had been actually *convicted* of a crime; their only concern would be the likelihood that he would be convicted (of a different crime) *in the future*, because *then* they'd have to pay the damages.[38]

This analysis also resolves the issue of parole. Although most crimes would involve financial restitution, rather than imprisonment, there would still be individuals who were too dangerous to

---

[37] I stress that cases like this are going to happen under *any* system. I am not conceding anything by admitting such possibilities; rather, I am trying to show the strength of my approach by explaining its *response* to such cases.

[38] Again, this process does *not* involve a violation of anyone's rights. It no more discriminates against clients than the present practice of charging young males higher car insurance premiums, even if their driving record is snow white. We don't need to fear a roundup of all mentally handicapped people, or all young black males, because such practices would not be profitable. If a certain individual were truly being charged a premium higher than he "deserved," he could shop around for a different insurance company.

be allowed loose. The insurance companies would determine this threshold. As long as a company were willing to pay for any damages a criminal might commit in the future, people would offer him work, let him rent a room, etc. Rehabilitation would thus be in the great financial interest of the companies, in order to increase their pool of paying customers.

On the other hand, truly dangerous individuals would not be "paroled." Right now, the government has psychologists and other "experts" decide when sex offenders and murderers should be let back on the streets. Since they have no accountability, these ivory tower intellectuals often test out their theories on the hapless victims of recidivist criminals.[39]

VI. CONCLUSION

This essay has outlined the mechanics of purely voluntary, market law. The main theme running throughout is that competition and accountability would force *true* experts to handle the important decisions that must be made in any legal system. It is a statist myth that justice must be produced by a monopoly institution of organized violence.

The arguments of this essay are admittedly incomplete; surely more thought is needed before a move to market anarchy becomes feasible. However, I ask that the reader resist the temptation to dismiss my ideas as "unworkable," without first specifying in what sense the *government* legal system "works."

---

[39] When I watch *America's Most Wanted* or read books explaining how the FBI catches serial killers, I am shocked by how many current murderers and rapists commit their crimes while on parole.

Illustration: Robert Vroman

Private Defense

Virtually everyone agrees that a government is needed to provide the essential service of military defense. People with an open mind may be genuinely sympathetic to the arguments for a free society. Yet they regard all the clever blueprints for an anarchist social order as hopelessly naïve, because a community based on voluntary relations would apparently be helpless in the face of neighboring States.

This essay claims that such a view, though widespread, is completely false. There is nothing intrinsic to military defense that requires State provision. The free market can provide defense more cheaply and more effectively than the government can. It is foolish and reckless to entrust the State with the protection of civilian lives and property. Private defense forces would enjoy a tremendous advantage, and in all but the most lopsided contests would slaughter their government adversaries.

I. INSURANCE

In an anarchist society committed to the sanctity of private property and contract, insurance companies would most likely oversee defense services.[40] To see how this market would operate, an analogy will be useful.

---

[40] This is the standard view among anarcho-capitalist writers. See for example Linda and Morris Tannehill, *The Market for Liberty* (New York: Laissez-Faire Books, 1984); Murray N. Rothbard, *For a New Liberty* (New York:

Imagine a large city located on a major fault line. Every so often, the residents endure a severe earthquake, which kills dozens of people and causes billions of dollars in property damage. To cope with the risk of such disasters, people purchase insurance for their lives and property. Policyholders pay a fixed premium, while the insurance agencies pledge to indemnify the estates of anyone who suffers bodily or financial harm during an earthquake, according to the precise terms specified in the contract.

The force of competition keeps the price of such insurance reasonable. Actuaries can estimate the expected costs per period of providing certain levels of coverage, and thus calculate the minimum premiums that would allow the insurer (all things considered) to break even in the long run. If the market rates exceed these minimum prices, new firms will have an incentive to enter the insurance market to reap the profits. Their entry would drive insurance premiums down towards the actuarially fair rates.

It is crucial to realize that the behavior of the residents greatly influences the city's vulnerability to earthquakes, and thus the total bill paid out by insurance companies following each disaster. Buildings, roads, and bridges can be designed with varying degrees of structural integrity and construction costs; the better the design, the greater its expense. Through their premium structure, insurance companies provide incentives for safer designs, thus defraying their higher costs. Profit-hungry businesses will thereby produce buildings and infrastructure exhibiting the optimal combination

---

Collier, 1978); and Hans-Hermann Hoppe, "The Private Production of Defense," *Journal of Libertarian Studies* 14:1 (Winter 1998–1999), esp. pp. 35–42. Even though these thinkers have outlined a feasible mechanism for private defense, insurance companies may not be the vehicle actually used in a real anarchist society: there could exist an even *better* market solution, yet to be imagined.

of durability and price,[41] without any need for government codes and inspectors.

In addition to encouraging sturdier designs, insurance companies could use other means to reduce their exposure. They might employ teams of seismologists to forecast earthquakes and publicize these findings as a service to their customers. For those clients too poor to afford housing in quake-proof buildings, the insurance companies can construct shelters, and require that these policyholders evacuate their buildings and retire to the shelters in an emergency.[42] In general, an insurance company will gladly spend funds to protect its clients and their property, so long as the expected reduction in liability claims is sufficient to justify the expenditure.

Just as the free market can provide the optimal response to dangerous earthquakes, so too can it provide the best protection from foreign militaries. Like natural disasters, wars bring widespread

---

[41] Suppose there are two construction firms, Shady and Reliable, and that there is one major earthquake per year. A bridge designed by Shady costs only $10 million, but in the event of an earthquake will collapse 10 percent of the time. A bridge designed by Reliable, on the other hand, costs $15 million but during an earthquake has only a 1 percent chance of collapsing. (Assume the bridges are identical in all other relevant respects.) The annual policy ensuring a Shady bridge would be priced at roughly $1 million, while the premium for a Reliable bridge would be roughly $150,000. So long as the interest rate is no higher than approximately 20 percent, the savings on insurance premiums justify purchasing the safer (yet more expensive) Reliable bridge. (For simplicity, we have ignored depreciation of aging bridges, the time it takes to rebuild a collapsed bridge, and the liability claims from killed customers.) Note that this preference for the safer design has nothing to do with altruism on the part of bridge owners, who are merely trying to minimize their costs.

[42] The precise arrangement would be specified contractually. For example, an insurance policy might require that clients tune in to a certain TV or radio station during an emergency, and follow the instructions. Of course, the clients would be free to disregard these warnings and remain in their (relatively unsafe) homes, but would thereby forfeit any compensation should they suffer personal injury during the quake.

death and destruction. In market anarchy, insurance companies would provide coverage for these losses too, and would thus have a great financial interest in deterring and repelling military attacks.

II. FINANCING

It is easy enough to imagine a system of private mail delivery or even highway construction. In contrast, free market defense presents a conceptual hurdle, since it is not clear what would be the voluntary analogs to government taxation and military spending.

Defense from foreign aggression is a classic "public good" and as such seems the perfect candidate for government provision.[43] Without the ability to extort revenues from all citizens, how could private firms raise the funds required by modern militaries? (After all, any individual citizen could refuse to buy the "product," yet still enjoy the security made possible by his neighbors' contributions.) On a practical level, hundreds of small, decentralized armies would surely be wiped out by a consolidated attack from a neighboring State.

The framework described in the first section avoids these apparent difficulties. In a free society, it is not the average person, but rather the *insurance companies*, that would purchase defense services. Every dollar in damage caused by foreign aggression would be fully compensated, and thus insurers would seek to protect their customers' property as if it were their own.[44] Because of economies of scale, coverage for large geographical regions would likely be handled through a few dominant firms, ensuring standardized pricing and a coordinated defense.

---

[43] In mainstream economic literature, a *public good* is both non-excludable and non-rival in consumption. In other words, the seller of a public good can't limit it to paying customers, and one person can consume the good without reducing its availability to another. Clean air is a prototypical public good.

[44] In economist jargon, the insurance agencies would internalize the positive externalities (among their customers) of defense spending.

It will be useful to elaborate on this hypothetical consolidation. Suppose we start in an initial anarchist society with no defense services at all. Imagine that the one serious military threat is invasion and conquest by a certain mercurial neighbor. The residents of this free society take out insurance policies on their lives and all major property, such that the total claims that would follow an invasion are estimated at one trillion dollars.[45] The insurance agencies hire geopolitical consultants and believe that the annual risk of attack is ten percent. They must therefore collect roughly $100 billion per year in premiums to cover themselves. If the society is composed of ten million people, the per capita expenditure on insurance from foreign aggression is $10,000. On top of this hefty expense, the residents remain completely vulnerable.

In this bleak situation, an executive at the Ace insurance company has a brilliant idea. He can undercut his rivals and offer the same level of coverage for only, say, $5,000 per person—half the price charged by his competitors. He can afford to do this by spending some of his revenues on military defenses, and thereby *lower* the probability of foreign conquest. For example, he might pay private defense agencies $40 billion per year to maintain helicopters, tanks, trained personnel, etc. and be on the constant alert to repel any attacks. If these preparations reduced the chance of foreign invasion to only, say, one-half of one percent per year, then they would "pay for themselves." The innovative insurance executive would reap huge profits and capture the market for military liability, while the residents would enjoy increased security and lower premiums. With

---

[45] Such a scenario raises an interesting question: Why would people buy insurance from foreign conquest? What good is it to receive a check for damaged property if it too would be confiscated? One possible market response would be to diffuse ownership over large areas. For example, real estate agencies would own property in every major city, rather than concentrating it in one area. Investment firms would consider a financial asset's "location" when assembling their diversified portfolios. In this way, even if a free society fell entirely to a State, the (multinational) insurance companies would still need to indemnify the absentee owners of much of the seized property.

property safe from foreign expropriation, investment and population growth would be stimulated, allowing greater economies of scale and further rate cuts.

Free Riders

Does the above system really avoid the perennial problem of private defense? That is, can it overcome the "free rider" problem? After Ace Insurance entered into long-term contracts with defense agencies, what would stop a rival firm, such as Moocher Insurance, from undercutting Ace? After all, the likelihood of property damage would be the same for Moocher's clients as for Ace's, yet Moocher wouldn't spend a dime on military expenditures.

This reasoning is perfectly valid, yet the case for private defense remains strong. In the first place, the clients of the insurance companies are not homogeneous, and consequently the market for defense is far more "lumpy" than assumed in standard economic models. Although above we discussed per capita premiums, this was only to give the reader a rough idea of the expenses involved. In reality, large firms would provide the bulk of revenue for the insurance industry. The policies taken out on apartment complexes, shopping malls, manufacturing plants, banks, and skyscrapers would dwarf those taken out by individuals.

Consequently, there wouldn't be the nightmarish bargaining problem that so worries the skeptics of private defense. The brilliant executive at Ace Insurance would be perfectly aware of the above considerations. If necessary, he would write only long-term contracts, and would make them conditional on the acceptance of a minimum threshold of clients. In other words, he would offer a package deal to the major companies, but the special, low rates would only apply if a sufficient number of these policies were sold.

It is true that this suggested remedy is rather vague. There are many interesting issues (studied in cooperative game theory) concerning the bargaining process of these large firms, and how the costs of defense *would* be split among them. But make no mistake, military defense would be adequately funded, for the simple reason that shareholders of rich companies are anything but reckless when it comes to money. Because of their size, the biggest companies couldn't ignore the effect of their own behavior on military preparedness.[46]

Furthermore, certain types of property—airports, bridges, highways, power plants, and of course, military equipment—would be far likelier targets of foreign attack, and their owners would thus constitute an even *smaller* group to benefit disproportionately from defense expenditures. This heterogeneity would weaken further the "spillover" character of defense services, making an efficient arrangement all the easier to achieve. Those companies that ended up paying the most might perceive the arrangement as unfair, but there would nevertheless always *be* an arrangement.[47] The highest contributors might even advertise this fact, much as large corporations make ostentatious donations to charity in order to curry goodwill.

Thus we see that the "lumpiness" of a realistic defense industry mitigates the impact of the positive externalities (spillover effects) of military spending. Because a few critical industries will pay for a basic level of defense regardless of contributions from others, the only possible harm of free riding would be an "unfair" burden placed on certain corporations. In any event, it isn't obvious that there would even *be* widespread free riding. As we shall now argue, defense services can largely be restricted to paying customers, after all.

---

[46] Even Moocher Insurance would recognize the dangers of luring too many of these big customers from Ace, since Moocher's premiums would be based on the accustomed level of security provided by Ace's defense spending.

[47] The typical economist who explains why the free rider problem renders private defense impractical *also* argues that cartels are inherently unstable because of incentives for cheating. Yet the countries of OPEC always manage to reach an agreement to limit output and distribute the gains.

In the earlier discussion, we treated a foreign invasion as an all-or-nothing proposition; the neighboring State either quickly conquered the anarchist society or was effectively deterred from attacking. In reality, wars can remain in stalemate for many years. During such protracted struggles, insurance companies would certainly be able to deploy their military forces so as to limit gratuitous protection for non-clients.

Most obvious, naval escorts would only protect convoys of paying customers. All other shipping would be at the mercy of foreign fleets. Antiaircraft and missile defenses would only protect those regions in which paying customers owned property. And of course, the owners of real estate on the border would always pay for its protection, lest the defense agencies pull their tanks and troops back to a more defensible position.[48]

Government vs. Private Military Expenditures

The above considerations show that people living in market anarchy could overcome the free rider problem and raise funds adequate for their defense. Yet there is a symmetric counterargument that is generally overlooked. It is true that coercive taxation allows governments to acquire immense military budgets. But this advantage is more than offset by the tendency of governments to squander their resources. For any meaningful comparison between government and private defense budgets, the latter needs to be multiplied severalfold, since private agencies can purchase equivalent military hardware at only a fraction of the prices paid by governments.

---

[48] In the extreme, we can even imagine defense agencies providing explicit intelligence to foreign enemies, specifying which neighborhoods could be bombed without reprisal. The statist commanders—perhaps after verifying that such reports didn't constitute a trap—would be delighted to adjust their attacks, since this would allow them to achieve their objective, i.e., carnage, with less resistance.

Everyone knows that governments are profligate with their money, and that military budgets are always a huge component of total spending. Since their operations are often conducted in foreign lands and shrouded in secrecy, a military can spend its funding with virtually no accountability. Taxpayers were shocked when an audit revealed that the U.S. Pentagon had spent $600 per toilet seat. What few people realize is that this example is *typical*. Because of the government's monopoly, no one has any idea how much an F-14 Tomcat "should" cost, and so *its* $38 million price tag shocks no one.

This last point is important, so I want to stress that it is caused by the very nature of government, not merely the accidents of history. If a government raises its funds through taxation, then it must *justify* this theft by spending the money on "the public good." Except in the most despotic regimes, the rulers can't simply pocket the money. Consequently, not a single official in the entire government has any personal incentive to identify and eliminate wasteful spending.[49]

In market anarchy, on the other hand, defense services would be sold in the open market. Fierce competition among suppliers and cost consciousness among the buyers would keep the prices of toilet seats as well as fighter jets as low as possible.

III. ECONOMIC CALCULATION

The first two sections demonstrated that military defense, like any other service, can be provided on the free market. To appreciate the tremendous advantage that this gives to the anarchist society, it will be useful to first explore the peacetime superiority of private industry versus government planning. To this end, we will review the critique of socialism.

---

[49] The use of audits only pushes the problem back one step. Government auditors are under far less pressure than private sector ones, since their employers—the legislators—do not desire frugality, but only the *appearance* of frugality to the taxpayers.

The traditional opponents of socialism argued that it had insufficient incentives for the average worker; without tying pay to performance, people would shirk and output would be far lower than in a capitalist economy. Only if a new "Socialist Man" evolved, who enjoyed working for his comrades as much as for himself, could a socialist system succeed. Although valid, this criticism misses the essence of the problem. It took Ludwig von Mises to explain,[50] in a 1920 paper, the true flaw with socialism: Without market prices for the means of production, government planners cannot engage in economic calculation, and so literally *have no idea* if they are using society's resources efficiently. Consequently, socialism suffers not only from a problem of incentives, but also from a problem of knowledge.[51] To match the performance of a market economy, socialist planners would not need to be merely angels, committed to the commonweal—they would also need to be gods, capable of superhuman calculations.

At any time, there is only a limited supply of labor, raw materials, and capital resources that can be combined in various ways to create output goods. A primary function of an economic system is to determine which goods should be produced, in what quantities and in what manner, from these limited resources. The market economy solves this problem through the institution of private property, which implies free enterprise and freely floating prices.

The owners of labor, capital, and natural resources—the "means of production"—are free to sell their property to the highest bidder. The entrepreneurs are free to produce and sell whatever goods they wish. The ultimate test of profit and loss imposes order on this seeming chaos: If a producer consistently spends more on his

---

[50] For a fuller discussion, see Ludwig von Mises, *Socialism: An Economic and Sociological Analysis* (Indianapolis: Liberty Fund, 1981).

[51] Strictly speaking, the "knowledge problem" (stressed by Friedrich Hayek) is not quite the same as the more general calculation problem, but the difference lies outside the scope of this essay.

inputs than he earns from selling his output, he will go bankrupt and no longer have any influence on the manner in which society's resources are used. On the other hand, the successful producer creates value for consumers, by purchasing resources at a certain price and transforming them into goods that fetch a higher price. In the market economy, such behavior is rewarded with profits, which allow the producer in question to have a greater say in the use of society's scarce resources.

None of this is true in the socialist state. Even if they truly intended the happiness of their subjects, the government planners would squander the resources at their disposal. With no test of profit and loss, the planners would have no feedback and would thus be operating in the dark.[52] A decision to produce more shoes and fewer shirts, or vice versa, would be largely arbitrary. Furthermore, the individuals to ultimately decide the fate of society's resources would be selected through the political process, not through the meritocracy of the market.

IV. PRIVATE vs. GOVERNMENT DEFENSE

The general advantages of private industry over government planning operate just as well in the field of military defense. Because the military derives its funding in a coercive manner, the link between output and consumer satisfaction is severed. Because of their monopoly, a State's armed forces can bumble along indefinitely, with no benchmark of comparison. Even in a limited State, whose subjects enjoy a large degree of economic freedom, the armed forces constitute an island of socialism.

To get a sense of the problems involved, imagine the situation faced by Josef Stalin during World War II. As absolute dictator,

---

[52] An example may illustrate the problem: Everyone knows that it would be incredibly "wasteful" to construct a bridge out of solid gold. Yet the vast majority of the planners' decisions—not only of *what* to make but *how* to make it—are not so obvious.

Stalin had at his disposal every resource—including human—in the Soviet Union. Stalin needed to use these resources to achieve his goals, the foremost of which (we shall assume) was the preservation and expansion of his political rule.

Some of Stalin's choices were obvious enough. Clearly he needed to overthrow the Nazi regime. And clearly *this* required (before their surrender) defeat of the German armies besieging Stalingrad.

As we become more specific, however, Stalin's choices become less clear. Yes, he should use all available steel for the production of military equipment; there is no need for new tractors at the moment. But how much of this steel should be devoted to planes? to tanks (and which models)? to mortars? to bombs? or to railroads (needed to move materiel to the front)?

Yes, all civilians—young and old, sick and healthy—should devote their lives to repelling the Huns. But precisely how many people should engage the enemy? work in tank factories? dig trenches around the city? or forage for food (to ensure survival through the winter)?

Even those tactical and strategic decisions normally made by military commanders have the same flavor. Yes, a sharpshooter such as Vasily Zaitsev should be used as a sniper, rather than as bomber pilot or factory worker. But how best to exploit Vasily? Should he be ordered to kill as many Germans as quickly as possible? Surely not, for with every shot he reveals his position. But it would also be far too conservative to have him wait months in the hopes of getting one clear shot at a general.

It is evident that Stalin (or his subordinates) must make all of these decisions and thousands more just like them largely through arbitrary guesswork. The wartime goal of expelling the enemy is no different from the peacetime problem of food production. In both cases, Stalin's actions led to the deaths of millions of his own people. Just as a free market in agriculture would have prevented famine, a free market in defense would have prevented such monstrous casualties.

Private Defense

Economic calculation allows entrepreneurs to judge whether a plan has been profitable. It allows successful ventures to expand and causes failed operations to disband. The market constantly readjusts itself to the changing data: conditions of supply, consumer demand, technical knowledge.

Now that we understand the manner in which insurance companies could objectively and quantitatively appraise military success, it is easy to see the advantages of private defense. In a situation comparable to the Battle of Stalingrad, the anarchist community would respond in the most efficient manner humanly possible. Insurance companies would determine the relative value of various military targets, and place bounties on them (for capture or elimination). Individuals left to their own spontaneous devices would try various techniques to produce this "service." Some might buy tanks and hire men to attack the Germans head-on; others might hire sharpshooters to snipe at them from afar. Some might buy mortars and shell them. Some might hire propagandists and offer bribes to lure defectors.

Over time, only the best defense firms would survive. They would expand their operations, increasing the overall efficiency of the war effort. Because they would be operating in a system of property rights, they would need to purchase all of their resources, including labor. This would ensure that the resources were being used as effectively as possible. (For example, those areas on the front in urgent need of soldiers or ammunition would bid up their wages or prices, avoiding the arbitrariness of government troop deployment and supply.) Even if—to reduce transaction costs and maximize response time—a single firm monopolized the defense of a region, the firm could still engage in internal cost accounting and calculate the profitability of its various branches.

Perhaps more important, *free competition* would ensure that technological and strategic advances were rewarded and quickly implemented. In contrast, a government military must rely on a bureaucratic chain of command where innovation, especially from outsiders, is stifled. In a very real sense, a military confrontation between a statist and a free society would be a war of a few minds versus millions.

Apples and Oranges

This theoretical discussion is sure to provoke the cynic to remark, "I'd like to see what your insurance companies would do if they met a Panzer division."

But such a question misses the point. We have demonstrated that a private defense system is the most effective, not that it is invulnerable. Yes, a small society of anarchists would be unable to repel the total might of Nazi Germany. But a small society of *statists* would fare even worse—and in fact, plenty of government militaries *were* obliterated by Hitler's armies.

Expertise

One might wonder whether private individuals would be as knowledgeable about military affairs as government professionals. Surely Colin Powell makes a better general than Bill Gates.

This fact rests on the monopoly status of the U.S. military. If private individuals were allowed to *compete* with Pentagon generals, the incompetence of the latter would be manifest. The average stockholder is no expert in professional sports or foreign cuisine, yet private ownership still yields excellent baseball clubs and French restaurants. Savvy executives hire *others* to identify talented individuals.

Intelligence

Even if a military bound by property rights and contract would have fared well in wars of an earlier era, what of modern warfare, with its sophisticated espionage? Could there be anarchist spies?

Private defense agencies would gather research just as any company does. They would hire analysts and collect information in any way legally possible. Presumably the most powerful computers and smartest code breakers would reside in an anarchist society. Whatever (if any) the loss caused by prohibitions on wiretaps and torture, it would be more than recovered in efficiency.[53]

On this topic, we note that *counterintelligence* would probably be quite limited. Defense agencies would have (possibly) several major buyers and would be operating in an open market. Consequently, they would need to *advertise* the capabilities of their products. This openness, however, is a virtue: What better way to avoid military defeat than by showing potential enemies how *advanced* their anarchist foe would be? The defense agencies in a free society would have nothing to hide from governments.[54]

"Do or Die"

The nature of military defense makes it less amenable to the trial and error correction mechanism of the free market. A nation can spend years in preparation for an attack, without receiving any feedback on the quality of its efforts. A sudden invasion could then wipe out the private defenders before they had a chance to adapt. This situation is different from the typical industry, in which repeated transactions day in and day out

---

[53] The CIA, despite its sweeping powers and immense budgets, failed to predict the collapse of the Soviet Union, harbored a mole for years, caused the accidental bombing of the Chinese Embassy, and failed to prevent the 9/11 attacks (despite the discovery of similar terrorist plans as early as 1995).

[54] Certain precautions would obviously be taken. For example, a factory owner wouldn't hire an enemy diplomat for fear of sabotage. But as factory owner such a policy is perfectly within his rights; he wouldn't need any special "wartime powers."

allow experimentation with various techniques and the weeding out of inefficiencies.

To meet this objection, we must remember that private defense agencies, unlike their government counterparts, need not be limited to regional clients. A multinational defense agency[55] could provide, say, fighter jet services to several insurance companies in various areas of the world. Although inadequate strategies or training[56] might remain hidden until a sudden disaster, at most only one of the agency's "franchises" would be lost. The others would study the incident and learn to avoid it.

In such an environment, military strategists from all over the world would collaborate in the new art of defense. While government planners guarded their precious secrets and protocols, anarchist agencies would hire the best and brightest minds. Expert personnel would be rotated from region to region, providing training in the latest tactics and equipment.[57] High-tech weapons would be stockpiled in central locations, and loaned out to anarchist societies under imminent threat of attack. This sharing—unthinkable among government militaries except in the direst circumstances—would further reduce the costs of private defense.

---

[55] Hoppe writes, "[A]ll insurance companies are connected through a network of contractual agreements of mutual assistance and arbitration as well as a system of international reinsurance agencies, representing a combined economic power which dwarfs that of most if not all existing governments" (p. 36).

[56] Warren Earl Tilson II has proposed that private defense forces could maintain their edge by engaging in televised competition, a suggestion that would also ameliorate the funding problem. We note that (like professional sports) these contests would be fair, in sharp contrast to, say, the Pentagon's rigged ABM tests, on which billions of dollars of pork depend.

[57] It is true that government military officers engage in the same types of behavior, but on a far smaller scale than would be the case in a free market.

Nuclear Weapons

The case for private defense must deal with the possibility of nuclear blackmail. In modern warfare, it would seem that only a nation that can credibly threaten to obliterate its opponents is safe from a first strike.

The anarchist society would probably *not* develop or even own nuclear weapons. In the first place, the term *defense* has been adopted consciously in this essay, and is not the euphemism as used in government propaganda. Because they would gain nothing from foreign conquest—since this would constitute theft and would be fully prosecuted within the anarchist courts—the owners of defense agencies would have no *reason* to spend money on weapons that were ill-suited to tactical defense.[58] Precision of weaponry would be of paramount importance, since battles would be fought near or amidst a defense agency's customers.[59]

Another, perhaps more significant, consideration is that defense agencies would most likely be legally *prohibited* from owning "weapons of mass destruction." The anarchist legal system would operate on the same principles of voluntary contract that underlay the defense industry. Insurance companies would vouch for individuals and pledge to compensate anyone victimized by their clients. In an effort to limit their liability, insurers would require certain concessions from their customers. It is hard to imagine that an insurance agency would pledge, say, $1 million for any (innocent) person killed by Defense Firm X, when Firm X held a stockpile of hydrogen bombs.

---

[58] For example, would George W. Bush be spending $1 billion per month bombing caves in Afghanistan if it were *his* money?

[59] These considerations also show why an anarchist society need not fear a foreign government using their own (advanced) weaponry against them. Private defense firms would likely sell their wares to foreign buyers (depending on the legal status of governments in the anarchist courts), but these would be designed for defensive use. There would likely be no aircraft carriers, long-range bombers or subs capable of transoceanic voyages.

Despite its probable lack of nuclear weapons, the anarchist society remains a viable option. Most obvious, there are *statist* societies that currently survive without nuclear devices. By its very nature, the anarchist society would be a completely harmless neighbor.[60] No State would ever fear *attack* from an anarchist military, and so there would be no need to preemptively strike it (unlike the Japanese on Pearl Harbor). With no taxation, regulation, tariffs, or immigration quotas, the anarchist society would be of tremendous value to all major governments.[61] They would surely act to protect it from intimidation by a rival nuclear power.[62]

V. LESSONS FROM HISTORY

The historical record supports our theoretical discussion. Government military campaigns are characterized by gross blunders that would be comical if not so tragic.[63] The only reason certain powers,

---

[60] This of course implies that a *world* of anarchist societies would be free from war.

[61] The cynic may believe that major governments would perceive a successful anarchist society as a threat. Although this would be true to some extent, politicians aren't stupid; they rarely destroy lucrative trading partners, especially ones with the ability to defend themselves.

[62] This argument is admittedly an odd one; it seems to acknowledge the benefit of *some* coercive apparatus. But note how the critique has changed. Usually the critic of private defense says that it may work in theory but not practice. *Now* the critic complains that private defense may work in practice but not theory.

[63] General Washington's troops at Valley Forge were absurdly ill-equipped, many lacking shoes. During the Civil War, Union generals delayed the introduction of a newer rifle for fear their men would waste ammunition. Proponents of air power were ridiculed in the first World War. British admirals stubbornly refused to convoy their ships in response to German U-boats, until their U.S. allies convinced them otherwise. Maginot's Line proved to be a bad joke. The Polish army used cavalry against the blitzkrieging Germans, after telling its men the tanks were made of cardboard.

such as the United States, maintain their aura of dominance is that they only fight *other governments*.[64]

So far we have restricted attention to government militaries *per se*. In reality, of course, a State hampers *all* of its operations with wartime controls, further weakening its military effectiveness. Price controls cause not only consumer vexation—through ration cards and "Meatless Tuesdays"—but also reduce output.[65] Modern wars are won with material. It is no accident that the freest nations usually win their wars.

It is a statist myth that abuse of rights must be met in kind. Bertrand de Jouvenal in his classic *On Power* argues that the other European countries had no choice but to institute conscription in response to Napoleon.[66] Yet this example only proves the dismal imagination of government planners. Surely a resilient anarchist society would have used its superior technology and industrial capacity to furnish voluntary armies[67] with forts, cannons, horses,

---

The intelligence failures surrounding Pearl Harbor were so monumental as to lend credibility to conspiracy theorists. Silent Service captains learned in the early stages of World War II that, due to a problem in the pin mechanism, direct hits would fail to explode their torpedoes, and so they purposely aimed for glancing shots. The manufacturer managed to deny the problem for years before finally correcting it. Examples abound of military blunders.

[64] The inability of a coalition of the world's strongest governments to eliminate a single man—Osama bin Laden—after months of "resolve" underscores the limits of State power.

[65] Price controls are particularly disastrous for countries enduring a blockade. Without lucrative profits, why would smugglers risk confiscation or even death?

[66] Bertrand de Jouvenel, *On Power: The Natural History of Its Growth* (Indianapolis: Liberty Fund, 1993), p. 164.

[67] The use of paid soldiers, who viewed their work as just an occupational choice, would also avoid the dangers posed by standing armies, which governments inevitably use against their own subjects.

and protective armor, sufficient to repel more numerous yet ill-equipped and poorly trained conscripts.[68, 69]

The analogy of France fighting other European powers is inappropriate. If a government army ever attacked an anarchist society, the situation would be akin to the Vietnam War with the technological roles reversed. There would be a clash of cultures similar to the encounter between Pizarro and the Incan emperor Atahuallpa.[70]

The advantages of private property are as manifest in the production of defense services as with any other. There is nothing magical about government military forces; if they have fewer tanks and planes and an inferior organization, they will lose to their anarchist opponents. A tiny country such as Taiwan can outperform com-

---

[68] Conscription, far from being a valuable tool of governments, only allows them to squander their most precious resource. On paper, the Southern states should have easily survived Northern attacks. But their commanders—trained at West Point—eschewed ungentlemanly guerrilla tactics and instead rounded up their able-bodied men and marched them into Union guns. See Jeffrey Rogers Hummel, *Emancipating Slaves, Enslaving Free Men* (Chicago: Open Court, 1996), pp. 178–179.

[69] We also note the relative difficulty Napoleon would face in conquering an anarchist (versus statist) neighbor. With no centralized government, there is no institution with the authority to *surrender* to a foreign power (see Hoppe, p. 49). By creating a coercive apparatus of taxation and control over their subjects, the other European states made Napoleon's task that much easier. In contrast, it took the British years to subdue Ireland, with its decentralized institutions.

[70] In one of the most lopsided military victories in history, "Pizarro, leading a ragtag group of 168 Spanish soldiers, was in unfamiliar terrain, ignorant of the local inhabitants, completely out of touch with the nearest Spaniards… and far beyond the reach of timely reinforcements. Atahuallpa was in the middle of his own empire of millions of subjects and immediately surrounded by his army of 80,000 soldiers.… Nevertheless, Pizarro captured Atahuallpa within a few minutes after the two leaders first set eyes on each other." See Jared Diamond, *Guns, Germs, and Steel* (New York: W. W. Norton & Co., 1999), p. 68.

munist China in the economic arena. It could defend itself just as efficiently if its residents would only abandon their faith in government police and armies, and embrace total freedom.

Bibliography on Anarcho-Capitalism
Compiled by Hans-Hermann Hoppe

Here is the essential reading on anarcho-capitalism, which might also be called the natural order, private-property anarchy, ordered anarchy, radical capitalism, the private-law society, or society without a state. This is not intended to be a comprehensive list. Indeed, only English-language works currently in print or forthcoming are included.

I. Murray N. Rothbard and Austro-Libertarianism

At the top of any reading list on anarcho-capitalism must be the name Murray N. Rothbard. There would be no anarcho-capitalist movement to speak of without Rothbard. His work has inspired and defined the thinking even of such libertarians such as R. Nozick, for instance, who have significantly deviated from Rothbard, whether methodologically or substantively. Rothbard's entire work is relevant to the subject of anarcho-capitalism, but centrally important are:

The Ethics of Liberty, the most comprehensive presentation and defense of a libertarian law code yet written. Grounded in the tradition of natural law and in its style of axiomatic-deductive reasoning, Rothbard explains the concepts of human rights, self-ownership, original appropriation, contract, aggression, and punishment. He demonstrates the moral unjustifiability of the state, and offers smashing refutations of prominent limited-statist libertarians such as Ludwig von Mises, F.A. Hayek, I. Berlin, and Robert Nozick.

In *For A New Liberty* Rothbard applies abstract libertarian principles to solve current welfare-state problems. How would a stateless society provide for goods such as education, money, streets, police, courts, national defense, social security, environmental protection, etc.? Here are the answers.

Power and Market is the most comprehensive theoretical analysis of the inefficiencies and counterproductive effects of every conceivable form of government interference with the market, from price controls, compulsory cartels, anti-trust laws, licenses, tariffs, child labor laws, patents, to any form of taxation (including Henry George's proposed "single tax" on ground land).

Egalitarianism As a Revolt Against Nature is a marvelous collection of Rothbard essays on philosophical, economic, and historical aspects of libertarianism, ranging from war and revolution to kids' and women's liberation. Rothbard shows his intellectual debt both to Ludwig von Mises and Austrian economics (praxeology) and to Lysander Spooner and Benjamin Tucker and individualist-anarchist political philosophy. This collection is the best single introduction to Rothbard and his libertarian research program.

The four-volume *Conceived in Liberty* is a comprehensive narrative history of colonial America and the role of libertarian ideas and movements. Rothbard's magisterial two-volume *An Austrian Perspective on the History of Economic Thought* traces the development of libertarian economic and philosophical thought throughout intellectual history. *The Irrepressible Rothbard* contains delightful libertarian commentary on political, social, and cultural issues, written during the last decade of Rothbard's life.

Justin Raimondo has written an insightful biography: *Murray N. Rothbard: An Enemy of the State*.

The Austro-libertarian tradition inaugurated by Rothbard is continued by Hans-Hermann Hoppe. In *Democracy—The God That Failed* Hoppe compares monarchy favorably to democracy, but criticizes both as ethically and economically inefficient, and advocates a natural order with competitive security and insurance suppliers. He revises fundamental orthodox historical interpretations, and reconsiders central questions of libertarian strategy. *The Economics and Ethics of Private Property* includes Hoppe's axiomatic defense of the principle of self-ownership and original appropriation: anyone arguing against these principles is involved in a performative or practical contradiction.

The Myth of National Defense is a collection of essays by an international assembly of social scientists concerning the relationship between State and war and the possibility of non-statist property defense: by militias, mercenaries, guerrillas, protection-insurance agencies, etc.

II. Alternative Approaches to Anarcho-Capitalism

The following authors come to similar conclusions but reach them in different ways and varying styles. While Rothbard and Hoppe are natural-rightsers of sorts and praxeologists, there exist also utilitarian, deontic, empiricist, historicist, positivist, and plain eclectic defenders of anarcho-capitalism.

Randy E. Barnett's *The Structure of Liberty* is an outstanding discussion of the requirements of a liberal-libertarian society from the viewpoint of a lawyer and legal theorist. Heavily influenced by F.A. Hayek, Barnett uses the term "polycentric constitutional order" for anarcho-capitalism.

Bruce L. Benson's *The Enterprise of Law* is the most comprehensive empirical-historical study of anarcho-capitalism. Benson provides abundant empirical evidence for the efficient operation of market-produced law and order. Benson's sequel *To Serve and Protect* is likewise to be recommended.

David D. Friedman's *The Machinery of Freedom* presents the utilitarian case for anarcho-capitalism: brief, easy to read, and with many applications from education to property protection.

Anthony de Jasay favors a deontic approach to ethics. His writing—in *The State*, in *Choice, Contract, Consent*, and the excellent essay collection *Against Politics*—is theoretical, with a neo-classical, game-theoretic flavor. Brilliant critic of public choice and constitutional economics—and the notion of minarchism.

Morris and Linda Tannehill's *The Market for Liberty* has a distinctly Randian flavor. However, the authors employ Ayn Rand's pro-state argument in support of the opposite, anarchistic conclusion. Outstanding yet much neglected analysis of the operation of competing security producers (insurers, arbitrators, etc.).

III. Precursors of Modern Anarcho-Capitalism

The contemporary anarcho-capitalist intellectual movement has a few outstanding nineteenth and early-twentieth century precursors. Even when sometimes deficient—the issue of ground land ownership in the tradition of Herbert Spencer and the theory of money and interest in the Spooner-Tucker tradition—the following titles remain indispensable and largely unsurpassed. (This listing is chronological and systematic, rather than alphabetical.)

Gustave de Molinari's pathbreaking 1849 article *The Production of Security* is probably the single most important contribution to the modern theory of anarcho-capitalism. Molinari argues that monopoly is bad for consumers, and that this also holds in the case of a monopoly of protection. Demands competition in the area of security production as for every other line of production.

Herbert Spencer's *Social Statics* is an outstanding philosophical discussion of natural rights in the tradition of John Locke. Spencer defends the right to ignore the state. Also highly recommended are his *Principles of Ethics*.

Auberon Herbert is a student of Spencer. In *The Right and Wrong of Compulsion by the State*, Herbert develops the Spencerian idea of equal freedom to its logically consistent anarcho-capitalist end. Herbert is the father of Voluntaryism.

Lysander Spooner is a nineteenth-century American lawyer and legal theorist. No one who has read "No Treason," included in *The Lysander Spooner Reader*, will ever see government with the same eyes. Spooner makes mincemeat of the idea of a social contract.

A concise history of individualist-anarchist thought and the related movement in nineteenth-century America, with particular attention to Spooner and Benjamin Tucker, is James J. Martin's *Men Against the State*.

Franz Oppenheimer is a left-anarchist German sociologist. In *The State* he distinguishes between the economic (peaceful and productive) and the political (coercive and parasitic) means of wealth acquisition, and explains the state as instrument of domination and exploitation.

Albert J. Nock is influenced by Franz Oppenheimer. In *Our Enemy, the State* he explains the anti-social, predatory nature of the state, and draws a sharp distinction between government as voluntarily acknowledged authority and the State. Nock in turn influenced Frank Chodorov, who would influence young Murray Rothbard. In his *Fugitive Essays*, a collection of pro-market, anti-state political and economic commentary, Chodorov attacks taxation as robbery.

IV. Congenial Writings

While not directly concerned with the subject of anarcho-capitalism and written by less-than-radical libertarian or even non-libertarian authors, the following are invaluable for a profound understanding of liberty, natural order, and the state.

John V. Denson's *The Costs of War* is a collection of essays by a distinguished group of libertarian and paleo-conservative scholars from various disciplines. Exposes the aggressive nature of the state. Possibly the most powerful anti-war book ever. Also to be recommended is Denson's collection *Reassessing the Presidency* on the growth of state power.

David Gordon's *Secession, State, and Liberty* is a collection of essays by contemporary philosophers, economists, and historians in defense of the right to secession.

Friedrich A. Hayek, *Law, Legislation, and Liberty*, Vol. I, is an important study on the "spontaneous" evolution of law, and the distinction of law versus legislation and between private and public law.

Bertrand de Jouvenel, *On Power*, is an outstanding account of the growth of state power, with many important insights concerning the role of the aristocracy as defender of liberty and mass democracy as a promoter of state power. Related, and likewise to be recommended is his *Sovereignty*.

Étienne de la Boétie, *The Politics of Obedience*, is the classic sixteenth-century inquiry into the source of government power. La Boétie shows that the state's power rests exclusively on public "opinion." By implication, every state can be made to crumble—instantly and without any violence—simply by virtue of a change in public opinion.

Bruno Leoni, *Freedom and the Law*, is an earlier and in some regards superior treatment of topics similar to those discussed by Hayek. Leoni portrays Roman law as something discovered by independent judges rather than enacted or legislated by central authority—and thus akin to English common law.

Robert Nisbet, *The Quest for Community* (formerly published under the more descriptive title Community and Power) explains the protective function of intermediate social institutions, and the tendency of the state to weaken and destroy these institutions in order to gain total control over the isolated individual.

The Journal of Libertarian Studies. An Interdisciplinary Quarterly Review, founded by Murray N. Rothbard and now edited by Hans-Hermann Hoppe, is an indispensable resource for any serious student of anarcho-capitalism and libertarian scholarship.

The following *JLS* articles are most directly concerned with anarcho-capitalism.

Anderson, Terry, and P.J. Hill, "The American Experiment in Anarcho-Capitalism," 3, 1.

Barnett, Randy E., "Whither Anarchy? Has Robert Nozick Justified the State?," 1, 1.

———, "Toward a Theory of Legal Naturalism," 2, 2.

Benson, Bruce L., "Enforcement of Private Property Rights in Primitive Societies," 9,1.

———, "Customary Law with Private Means of Resolving Disputes and Dispensing Justice," 9,2.

———, "Reciprocal Exchange as the Basis for Recognition of Law," 10, 1.

———, "Restitution in Theory and Practice," 12, 1.

Block, Walter, "Free Market Transportation: Denationalizing the Roads," 3, 2.

———, "Hayek's Road to Serfdom," 12, 2.

Childs, Roy A. Jr., "The Invisible Hand Strikes Back," 1,1.

Cuzan, Alfred G., "Do We Ever Really Get Out Of Anarchy?," 3, 2.

Davidson, James D., "Note on Anarchy, State, and Utopia," 1, 4.

Eshelman, Larry, "Might versus Right," 12, 1.

Evers, Williamson M., "Toward a Reformulation of the Law of Contracts," 1, 1.

———, "The Law of Omissions and Neglect of Children," 2, 1.

Ferrara, Peter J., "Retribution and Restitution: A Synthesis," 6, 2.

Fielding, Karl T., "The Role of Personal Justice in Anarcho-Capitalism," 2, 3.

Grinder, Walter E., and John Hagel, III, "Toward a Theory of State Capitalism," 1, 1.

Hart, David M., "Gustave de Molinari and the Anti-Statist Liberal Tradition," 3 parts, 5, 3 to 6, 1.

Hoppe, Hans-Hermann, "Fallacies of Public Goods Theory and the Production of Security," 9, 1.

———, "Marxist and Austrian Class Analysis," 9, 2.

———, "The Private Production of Defense," 14, 1.

Kinsella, N. Stephan, "Punishment and Proportionality," 12, 1.

———, "New Rationalist Directions in Libertarian Rights Theory," 12, 2.

———, "Inalienability and Punishment," 14, 1.

Liggio, Leonard P., "Charles Dunoyer and French Classical Liberalism," 1, 3.

Mack, Eric, "Voluntaryism: The Political Thought of Auberon Herbert," 2, 4.

McElroy, Wendy, "The Culture of Individualist Anarchism in Late 19th-Century America," 5, 3.

McGee, Robert W., "Secession Reconsidered," 11, 1.

Osterfeld, David, "Internal Inconsistencies in Arguments for Government: Nozick, Rand, Hospers," 4, 3.

———, "Anarchism and the Public Goods Issue: Law, Courts, and the Police," 9, 1.

Paul, Jeffrey, "Nozick, Anarchism, and Procedural Rights," 1, 4.

Peden, Joseph R., "Property Rights in Celtic Irish Law," 1, 2.

Peterson, Steven A., "Moral Development and Critiques of Anarchism," 8, 2.

Raico, Ralph, "Classical Liberal Exploitation Theory," 1, 3.

Rothbard, Murray N., "Robert Nozick and the Immaculate Conception of the State," 1, 1.

——, "Concepts of the Role of Intellectuals in Social Change Toward Laissez Faire," 9, 2.

——, "Nations by Consent: Decomposing the Nation-State," 11, 1.

Sanders, John T., "The Free Market Model versus Government: A Reply to Nozick," 1, 1.

Smith, George H., "Justice Entrepreneurship in a Free Market," 3, 4 (with comments by Steven Strasnick, Robert Formani and Randy Barnett and a reply by Smith, in the same issue).

Sneed, John D., "Order without Law: Where will Anarchists Keep the Madmen?," 1, 2.

Stringham, Edward, "Market Chosen Law," 14, 1.

Tinsley, Patrick, "Private Police: A Note," 14,1.

Watner, Carl, "The Proprietary Theory of Justice in the Libertarian Tradition," 6, 3–4.